Front Cover Calligraphy supplied by Eduardo Patrizio

All the things — All the time! ♡

JU NO SEIGO

Suppleness Will Overcome Strength

An introduction to the Japanese Martial Art of Jujutsu

Acknowledgements

I'd like to thank my instructors (past and present) for the knowledge they have imparted, and the opportunities I have had to train and learn.

I'd like to give special thanks to Yasumoto Akiyoshi, Motoha Yoshin Ryu Soke, for allowing me to use images of him in the publishing of this book.

I would like to thank the students of my dojo for their continued hard work and dedication that keeps me on my toes, as well as my friends in Budo. In particular those that have helped in the creation of this book as photo subjects, by providing artwork, or most importantly acted as my own personal test subjects.

Finally I'd like to thank my Wife, for enduring the hardships of being a Martial Art widow at times, and supporting me along the way, especially while my attention has been focused on writing this book.

FORWARD ALWAYS; ALWAYS FORWARD →

TABLE OF CONTENTS

The author with Yasumoto Akiyoshi, Motoha Yoshin Ryu Soke, taken in the Farnham Dojo, 2016

About the author

I began training in martial arts at a young age. Initially practicing Judo, however with the popularity of Kung Fu movies in the 1980's I soon switched to Kung Fu. I started with Lau Gar Kuen under Kevin Brewerton, who was also well known as a Champion Kick Boxer of the time.

As a young adult I then practiced a modern style of Goshinjutsu under the late founder of the system Mike Johnson, as well as Wing Chun Kung Fu under Dave Fenton of MYS Wing Chun Academy.

I travelled to Northern China in 2007 where I studied Shaolin Lohan Fist, Sanda Boxing, Tai Chi, and Qi Gong, under Du Sifu (Shaolin Name: Shi Xing Heng, 34th Generation Shaolin Monk) and Su Sifu (Shaolin Name: Shi Xing Qing, 32nd Generation Shaolin Monk)

Looking for something more authentic in my Japanese martial art training I began studying Nihon Jujutsu with Tanemura Shoto's KJJR organisation (Kokusai Jujutsu Renmei). This included training in Koryu such as Hontai Takagi Yoshin Ryu and Asayama Ichiden Ryu, as well as Kenjutsu and Bojutsu. In 2010 I was given permission to teach the KJJR system.

After this I found I wasn't happy practicing multiple schools under the one heading, believing that you can't truly embed the core principles and techniques of a Ryu when constantly changing what you are practicing. Some people may fit with this approach, but it wasn't for me.

As a matter of luck, or perhaps fate, I came across an opportunity to learn Motoha Yoshin Ryu Jujutsu, a Menkyo Kaiden branch of the Hontai Yoshin Ryu, Takagi Ryu via Andy McCormack, British Sohonbu-Cho.

Now at the time of writing this I currently hold the rank of Chuden no Maki, awarded by Yasumoto Akiyoshi Soke. I am also Dojo Cho of the Southern England Yoshinkan Branch Dojo, based in Farnham, Surrey, where I practice and teach this school of Jujutsu.

In addition to this, I also practice the Muso Shinden Ryu school of Iaido.

The author with his children

Southern England Yoshinkan Branch Dojo

Dojo Training, 2015

The author with Yasumoto Sensei, Yonago, Japan, 2017

The author with Shigeyoshi Sensei, Yonago, Japan, 2017

The author with Du Sifu (Shi Xing Heng), Shandong, China, 2007

The author with different Makimono awarded to him

Dojo Training 2016

Introduction

OK, so I've done it..... Finally written a book....

This is intended as a training aid for my students, or in fact any students of Jujutsu who take an interest in it. Giving a basic introduction to the Japanese Martial Art of Jujutsu and a number of the concepts involved.

It's important to note that this is not an instruction manual, but rather a summary of a number of the key principles discussed in class with explanations to help understanding, as well as a number of photo's shared from my personal collection in order to underpin the book with the feeling of our Dojo.

Another point to note is that there are many schools of Jujutsu, with different ideas, strategies, ways of performing techniques, histories, etc. This book is written based on my understanding and experience, and is not necessarily reflective of others. We are each on our own path which is unique to us, so please read with an open mind, and consider any differences you come across as simply that.

The path is also never-ending and the content of this book is based on my understanding at this point in time. This may change in the future as I continue my own studies.

I have tried to keep the content easy to follow, and give readers a solid understanding across a range of concepts, both physical and mental, to lay a foundation for further study.

I really hope you enjoy reading this book!

History

Given the many different ways in which schools of martial arts have been realised and developed, the many different names used, the fact multiple arts we consider to be separate entities today would have all been practiced under one roof, I believe it impossible in my opinion to give a one size fits all history of Jujutsu, without being so vague that it loses all value in any case.

So rather than trying to give a general history of Jujutsu, I have written here a brief history of the Hontai Yoshin Ryu Takagi Ryu line, of which Motoha Yoshin Ryu is a Menkyo Kaiden branch.

While some of the history is well documented, much of the early history of this school has become interwoven with legend. There are therefore a number of variations and inaccuracies in the events of the time depending on which sources you are looking at. I have tried to give a simple account based on my own understanding, to help explain how a school may have developed and been passed down to the present day, not to claim this as absolute historical fact.

Other schools will of course have their own histories and stories that may be quite different, so please consider this simply as one example.

Samurai Armour on display at the Victoria & Albert Museum, London, England

Samurai Armour on display in Matsue Castle, Shimane, Japan

Iya Shrine, Matsue, Shimane, Japan

Hontai Yoshin Ryu, Takagi Ryu

Takagi Oriemon was born in Japan's early Edo period, some sources claim the year 1625 while others believe it was 1635. His father was Inatomo Shuzen, a Samurai retainer serving under Katakura Kojuro, the lord of Shiroishi, in the province of Oushuu. According to some sources he served as an instructor of Kenjutsu and Naginatajutsu.

Oriemon's childhood name was Umon. He was mild mannered, practiced Bujutsu from a young age, and was renowned for his unusual size and strength.

It is said that after a show of strength in which Umon greatly impressed Lord Katakura, he was reprimanded by his father for his showing off, and had his name changed to Takagi Oriemon. This was done with the lesson that Takagi (tall trees) can break if blown by a strong wind, where the willow tree is supple and will not be broken. Pride should not be taken in the size and strength he was merely born with, as this could easily be undone, in being humble and by practicing restraint he could become like the willow.

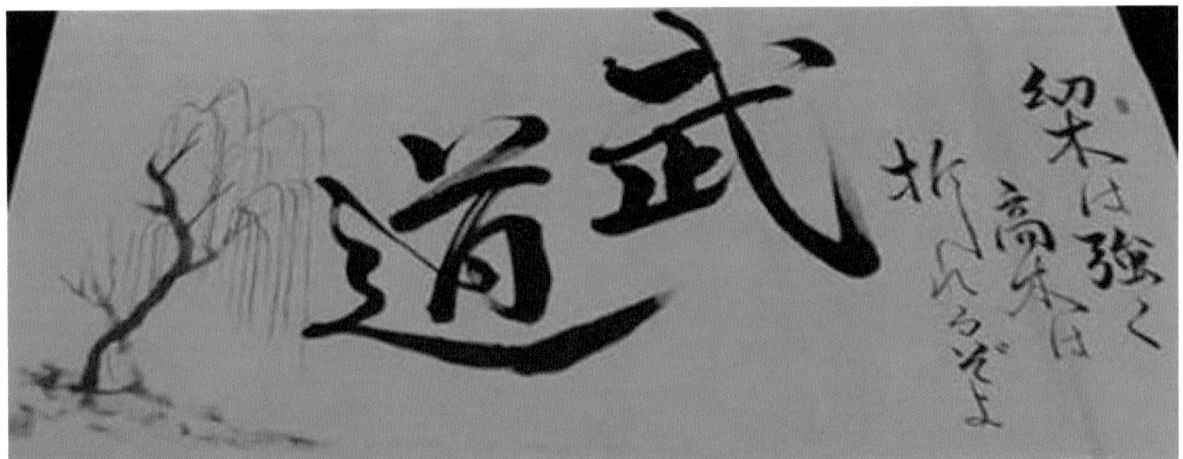

This beautiful artwork, highlighting the Willow Tree's connection to Budo as well as Inatomo Shuzen's lesson for his son, was created by Akemi Lucas - Koshu Japanese Art, who kindly gave it to me as a gift.

While Oriemon was proficient in multiple forms of Bujutsu, having learned from his father, as well as practicing under another instructor in the service of Lord Katakura, Ito Sasatada.* He took a journey of Musha Shugyo to seek out skilled teachers and hone his skills.

*Ito Sasatada was a retainer of Lord Katakura who taught a school he called Kenko Ryu.

The origins of Kenko Ryu seem to have been obscured in myth. Some sources claim Ito learned from a wandering monk named Unryu. Unryu is believed to have received transmission of an older form of Bujutsu, and to have been very skilled in a number of fighting arts, including Taijutsu.

While on Musha Shugyo, Oriemon took on a disciple, who he later adopted and gave the name Takagi Umanosuke. Umanosuke was also of large stature, and unusually strong.

Oriemon taught and eventually passed on to Umanosuke his system of fighting, developed from his existing martial training while applying his father's lesson. The system at this time is said to have consisted of Spear, Halberd, Gunnery, Short Sword, and Jujutsu.

It is recorded that Umanosuke later fought a duel with Takenouchi Hisayoshi, the third Soke of Takenouchi Ryu. Despite Umaosuke's size, strength, and martial skill, Hisayoshi defeated him easily and was able to bind him with a rope. Finding himself greatly impressed with Hisayoshi's skill he asked to be accepted as a student of Takenocuhi Ryu, and his request was accepted.

After achieving Menkyo Kaiden in Takenouchi Ryu, Umanosuke incorporated the lessons and strategies learned into the existing techniques of Takagi Ryu, and re-named the school Hontai Yoshin Ryu, Takagi Ryu. With Hontai Yoshin Ryu emphasising the suppleness of the willow tree, and how the techniques of the system do not rely on physical strength to make them work.

The school then passed to Takagi Gennoshin Hideshige, Umanosuke's son. During his time close links were made between the Hontai Yoshin Ryu, Takagi Ryu, and the Kukishin Ryu headed by Okuni Kihei Shigenobu.

It is said that following a duel, the two Soke decided to combine the schools, finding that the grappling techniques of the Hontai Yoshin Ryu, Takagi Ryu were superior, while the Kukishin Ryu staff was the better of the two. This blending of the schools was taken a step further when Takagi Gennoshin selected Okuni Kihei to succeed him as Soke.

Okuni Kihei was a samurai of the Ako domain, therefore these schools were then passed down together within the domain for a number of generations.

We then jump forward in time to around the end of the eighteenth century, and the thirteenth Soke, Yagi Ikugoro Hisayoshi. Losing his position within the Ako domain he decided to open a public dojo in order to maintain himself.

The fourteenth Soke, Ishiya (Ishitani) Takeo Masatsugu continued in this way and opened schools in a number of regions. He is said to have had great skill and was able to organise the school along with some additions of his own.

It is at this point where we really see some of the different branches of the school that exist today begin to take shape. While there were branches that had split before this point, the students of Ishiya Takeo seem to have been some of the most prevalent, the most famous of these branches in modern times (other than those of the main lineage) is that of his student Fujita Togoro Hisakichi, who is recorded as the teacher of Mizuta Hotaro Tadafusa, who in turn was a teacher of Takamatsu Toshitsugu. There are a number of schools practicing this line today, most notably the Bujinkan, Genbukan and Jinenkan organisations.

We then jump forward again to the early twentieth century and the sixteenth Soke of the main line, Kakuno Hachiheita Masayoshi, who broke with previous tradition and split the school. Minaki Saburoji was named seventeenth Soke of Hontai Yoshin Ryu, while Tsutsui Tomotaro became the seventeenth Soke of Takagi Ryu.

Minaki Soke then organised the system into new sets of Kata, still practiced today in the Hontai Yoshin Ryu mainline.

To understand where Motoha Yoshin Ryu then comes into play, Yasumoto Akiyoshi, was a student of Minaki Saburoji and also Kanazawa Ichizu who held Menkyo Kaiden in Takagi Ryu.

After receiving Menkyo Kaiden in both Takagi Ryu and Hontai Yoshin Ryu, Yasumoto Sensei later formed his own Ha of the school, reorganising the Kata and naming it Motoha Yoshin Ryu.

Motoha Yoshin Ryu

The Meaning of Jujutsu?

On the surface, Jujutsu is a term used to describe a set of Japanese martial arts, which focus on suppleness and yielding, rather than physical strength and opposing force, in order to overcome an opponent.

It is total body fighting, in that every part of the body can be used while applying joint manipulations, throws, strikes, chokes, and counter techniques to overcome an opponent.

 Ju   - Supple, Gentle, Yielding, Pliable

Jutsu   - Method, Technique, Art

A way of considering this is to look at how the Willow Tree moves in the wind. It is certainly not the

biggest or strongest tree, but by yielding to the winds power the Willow can withstand almost any storm.

If you look closely you will see that there is no resistance, as the wind blows one way, the branches flex and go that way, when the wind changes direction, so do the branches, continually yielding to the wind and therefore able to withstand the mightiest of storms without damage.

In winter, when other tree branches can become weighed down with snow and crack, the Willow will easily shrug such weight off sustaining no damage in the process.

This is 'Ju.'

Willow Trees, Tri-Lakes, Hampshire, England

If we then add to this the application of complimentary force to an opponent's movement in order to manipulate their structure and balance, gaining the advantage of a superior position, along with devastating methods of subduing the opponent, these are the methods of Jujutsu.

Different schools of Jujutsu will have their own ways of expressing this principle, and may differ greatly in their approach and their techniques, however what should be a constant factor is the element of not directly opposing force, or matching strength against strength in order to win.

'It is one of the traditional Japanese martial arts that do not require a weapon, or great strength, as even a weak person can perform the techniques. But it is a martial art for real fights, so practitioners naturally develop tougher bodies and greater patience and endurance.'
- Tanemura Shoto, KJJR Jujutsu Volume 1

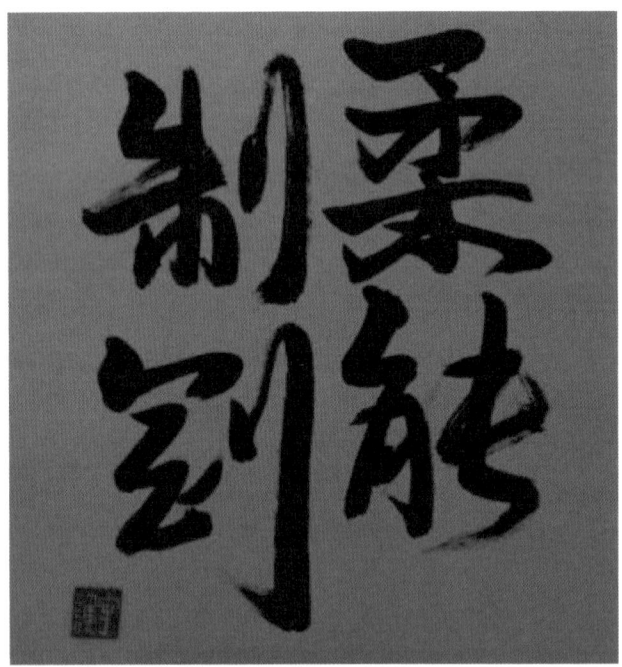

Ju no Seigo artwork brushed by my student Eduardo Patrizio

Ju no Seigo (Suppleness can overcome strength) a saying (and also the title of this book) captures the essence of Jujutsu. In being supple, and able to yield, the strongest person can throw all they have at you and find they are unable to cause damage.

If Jujutsu was only soft, or only ever yielded however, it would not be effective for real fighting. In reality there must be a balance, underpinning the soft elements there is a hardness of character, purpose, and will. Without these points people are really just playing at martial arts and not learning a true form of Budo.

Students practicing Takagi Ryu Jujutsu Kata, 2015

Classification

Schools of Jujutsu are often classified into 2 categories, Koryu or Gendai, explained below;

Koryu

Old Flow. This term is generally applied to schools of Japanese martial arts that were founded prior to the Meiji Restoration (1868) and the subsequent modernisation of Japanese society.

This term applies in the modern age to surviving Ryu, where direct transmission (flow) of the school has taken place and the lineage can be traced earlier than 1868.

Some of the oldest Jujutsu Koryu still alive today were founded almost 500 years ago (the Takenouchi Ryu for example was founded in the year 1532) however the origins of these schools date back even further than this, although their development prior to this time is often unclear.

Gendai

In comparison to Koryu, the term Gendai applies where a school has been created in the modern era, after 1868.

Many adhere rigidly to these classifications, and there are endless debates over whether certain schools are Koryu or not.

Now while I believe it is important to understand what you are practicing. If you are told that something is Koryu then you should be able to verify its authenticity. You should be able to verify the instructors' credentials. These are important factors, however I feel that often too much emphasis is placed on the specific date 1868, rather than the actual transmission or effectiveness of the school.

Transmission in my opinion is the most important thing to understand when considering a form of Jujutsu.

Can you see a line of transmission that connects your instructor to the founder of the school? This is not subjective, you either can or you can't, which is why I place a great deal of importance on this aspect.

For Koryu, does this line of transmission extend to a time when Samurai were active in Japan?

The date here becomes irrelevant in my opinion, as 1868 only really marked the beginning of the Meiji period. Samurai were still active in Japan after this date. It wasn't until 1876 that the law prohibiting the carrying of weapons in public was passed, this was the point at which Samurai really lost their special status.

Now even at this time Samurai didn't just disappear. They didn't lose all of their knowledge or abilities overnight. Some Samurai who had reached maturity before the Meiji period, were still around well into the early 1900's. Clothing may have changed, they may no longer have held special status, but any training they had undertaken, any knowledge gained was still with them.

The point here, is that regardless of the specific date, where you can see the line of transmission you can have a level of comfort that what you are being taught is authentic, even though some people may not consider the school Koryu.

The author teaching at charity Budo seminar 2017

Unarmed fighting

A common perception of Jujutsu that I don't subscribe to, is that of it being an 'unarmed' martial art. Especially when you consider the origins of the art.

Samurai by their very nature were very rarely unarmed, at the very least (even in peaceful times) they wore a pair of swords in their belts as a symbol of their social status, and that's without considering the various other weapons often carried or secreted about them. There was no practical need for any 'unarmed' system of fighting, everything was Bujutsu.

Fighting without a using weapon however is a very different to unarmed fighting. Even when wearing weapons there are times when their use is not possible or restricted, this is evident in a number of Jujutsu Kata where the goal is ultimately to clear a situation where a weapon could be drawn, or where the attack provided is intended to prevent a sword or other weapon from being brought to bear, or where parts of the weapon are even used to apply Jujutsu techniques.

While the difference between 'unarmed' and 'without using a weapon' may seem a very trivial point to discuss, I think it is an important definition when considering the finer points of Jujutsu, the strategy and mind set required.

The fact your opponent is carrying weapons will have a large impact on how you may attack them, your movement, the distancing you work to, and other factors. Allowing someone the chance to draw a blade is not a particularly good idea, the urgency you move with will therefore be far greater.

If we then consider the actual use of the Nihonto, it is designed as a two handed weapon* therefore to use it efficiently we have to have the full reach of both of our arms which will rely on having square hips, we also need to be able to move quickly in and out when attacking, so our posture must allow this.

*There are times when the Nihonto may be used one handed, however the general use and design of the weapon is to be wielded with both hands.

When practicing Koryu forms of Jujutsu, these points, as well as others should all be present in the training.

If you are anything like me, you may have spent time watching demonstrations of different schools, whether in person, on DVD, online or any other medium you could access. Something that was always clear to me, even at a time when I was practicing a modern form of Goshinjustu and was not familiar with Koryu, was the difference between the Japanese demonstrations, and those of western based systems.

The whole feel was completely different, I remember back then dismissing it as being purely a result of Japanese formality, but when I consider this now I see a whole different picture. I understand now, that what I was seeing or feeling when watching demonstrations of Japanese practitioners, was the spirit beyond the physical techniques, treating the opponent as though they had murderous intent, moving in a way that is covering against the use of weapons, but also in a way that emphasised efficient, natural movement. When watching the western based systems this just wasn't there.

Now this is a generalisation, and there are exceptions to this, but based on my own experiences and observations of the time, this was a clear difference, and had a very real impact on what was being shown.

The author with Makoto Kojima, Shuhan of Kishin Juku Aiki Jujutsu, 2014

Defence in Attack

Jujutsu is also spoken about, marketed and taught as a system of 'Self Defence.'

I've heard it said many times, by many different people, that the techniques of Jujutsu are all defensive. That by its very nature there must be an attack which can be yielded to. An opponent must exert a force to be manipulated, they must attack in order for Jujutsu to be applied.

I strongly disagree with this notion. I would even go as far as to say that this type of thinking is very dangerous, especially when considering a potentially violent encounter.

Waiting for someone to attack you, and purely reacting to that attack is generally a good way to get yourself hurt. It is certainly not a strategy that is going to put you at any advantage when fighting.

Unless you are very lucky, you will begin on the back foot and struggle to regain composure. This is one of the reasons I have often seen experienced martial artists lose in real fights with untrained people, this reactive strategy simply doesn't work in my opinion.

This type of reactive strategy is known as Go no Sen, and is often used for initial basic training, where students need to work around an attack to learn the shape of techniques before being able to apply a more pre-emptive strategy, Sen no Sen.

I believe this idea of Jujutsu for self defence to have become more prevalent in the late Edo period through to the present day. By the 1800's Tokugawa society had greatly reduced conflict in comparison to the past. Systems were therefore created and practiced in a time where many who trained in the Dojo never actually experienced real violence.

Often competitive fighting took the place of actual fighting, and required a different set of skills to those found in the older Koryu. A schools popularity and perceived effectiveness at this time was based more on the student's ability in these type of matches, than on the brutal efficiency of their forerunners.

This belies the often heard affirmation that only those schools that worked in battle survived. While I can certainly understand that being a possibility when talking about older Koryu, it would be very difficult to claim the same for those developed later.

If you think on it further, this idea of 'Self Defence' doesn't tie in with other Samurai originated martial arts.

'With your spirit calm, attack with a feeling of constantly crushing the enemy, from first to last. The spirit is to win in the depths of the enemy.'
– Miyamoto Musashi, Go Rin no Sho

Now I'm not saying in any way that Jujutsu isn't an effective method of Self Defence!

Quite the contrary, I personally believe it to be the most effective martial art available for this purpose and that is a big reason for my love of the art. I simply don't subscribe to the belief that Jujutsu is only defensive in nature, or has a strategy primarily focused on Self Defence.

Jujutsu to me, is a brutally effective method of fighting, offensive in strategy as much as defensive. With the primary focus on destroying or subduing your opponent quickly and efficiently.

Jujutsu therefore is intended to allow the practitioner to gain the upper hand in any encounter. Many other martial arts do this by training themselves to be as physically strong as possible, Jujutsu on the other hand should apply a strategy of yielding when appropriate, but also that of attack when the advantage can be gained.

The All Japan Kendo Federation vocalised this idea well I think in their publication, Fundamental Kendo. While they refer to the practice of Kendo, the theory I think carries across Budo as a whole.

'You must always realise that Kendo defence exists for the sake of attack and that Kendo attacks are a kind of self-defence.'

'Throughout repeated training sessions, cultivate the attitude that defence exists in attack and attack in defence. Gradually you will come to see that neither one exists apart from the other.'

- All Japan Kendo Federation, Fundamental Kendo

Satoshi Miyamura, Wakaba Kendo Club demonstration at Japan Matsuri, London, 2017

This also becomes clearer when we consider the techniques of Jujutsu holistically.

If we take for example attacks that involve grabbing a wrist. Now I often get upset when I watch these type of techniques and see them practiced with no intent or purpose. Uke just holding a wrist for the sake of it. I'm not referring to this type of practice here, but rather in the context of Uke having to pin the wrist to prevent Tori from being able to draw his sword.

This may be an offensive move (as is often practiced) where Uke is removing Tori's ability to draw his sword in defence, with the intention of continuing the attack.

This is the most common understanding or explanation I've heard from Jujutsu instructors over the years.

I think of it differently. While there is nothing wrong with this explanation, it is in truth a very narrow view and misses a number of factors. There could be other possibilities.

Imagine if you will, that Tori is actually the aggressor;

1. They decide to attack, and move to draw their sword with the intention of cutting Uke down, or they feign a movement to instigate Uke's reflex.

2. Seeing Tori's movement Uke reacts in defence, and springs to prevent the draw and gain control of Tori.

3. Tori uses Jujutsu to overcome Uke's defence and finish him off.

The same technique can be both attack and defence as the situation dictates. They are not independent of each other, but are really two sides of the same coin. Both utilise the same Jujutsu yielding principles based on the movements of the opponent, even when in an offensive position.

If we practice only the defensive side, or consider the art as being purely for defence, we are not practicing Jujutsu with the correct fighting spirit, and as a true fighting martial art. If we always train to act defensively, we are in truth training ourselves to lose.

A good fighter will take the initiative and exploit an opportunity. The ones who can do this will usually be the ones who come out on top regardless of any training undertaken or physical bulk.

Mind and Body

It is very easy when training and learning a martial art to fixate on the specific techniques you are learning. If you learn a way of striking, you fixate on that and think of how it can be used. If you learn a particular throw you fixate on that and think of how you may execute it in different scenarios. If you learn a joint lock you may think of numerous ways in which to enter that position. This is completely natural, especially when learning, but it is not really an appropriate approach when we come to consider the actual strategies of Budo.

I've found in my training history however that this approach is often encouraged in training. Syllabus are created based on responses to certain attacks, line ups or gauntlets are held, where students must defend against multiple attacks using different techniques to show their array of knowledge.

While this can be a great form of training to build stamina, or to perform techniques under pressure, it actually goes completely against the real strategy of Jujutsu, and the elements that actually make it an effective form of fighting.

You should train your body to be able to perform techniques in the correct manner, utilising the principles of the school, without thought, however you must also ensure you train your mind to the same extent.

The strategy of Jujutsu can only really be appreciated when you are able to perform the techniques in the correct way, along with combination of the three minds; Zanshin, Fudoshin, and Mushin.

Zanshin

Zanshin or Remaining Mind is likely the most important element to understand when practicing any form of Budo, this is what sets true martial artists aside from those that play at it.

I first came across this word in the context of awareness, after executing a technique being aware of surroundings and any potential further threat. Through my training, I now realise how limited that understanding of the concept was, really only barely scratching the surface.

Rather than only being aware, think of having a clear focus on the situation and a single minded determination to succeed. In this way, your opponents resolve can be shaken or even broken before any type of physical action happens.

This focus connects you and your opponent, they can sense it, everything in the moment should exude your determination to win, your clear focus, your posture and eyes reflecting your commitment and readiness to fight without let up. Here we also see the connection between Zanshin and Metsuke.

In his book Daito Ryu Aikijujutsu - Hiden Mokuroku: Ikkajo, Kondo Katsuyuki explains Zanshin as the idea of leaving nothing of the spirit behind, holding nothing back and putting everything you have into your technique.

When in this state you should immerse yourself fully into the fight as if your victory is already a forgone conclusion, this will prevent any hesitation to act when the time comes.

Throughout the whole encounter, remain focused, control your own spirit, calmly take in your opponent, your surroundings, each detail without conscious effort, and act without carelessness.

Think of this state as being like a notched arrow, clearly focused on the target, calm, string taut, aware of all around you but not distracted by it, confident in the fact that within a split second you can be released and spring forward with no hesitation to hit your mark.

When the spirit is completely immersed in the fight, connected to the moment with the unerring confidence and desire to succeed that let's your opponent know that you have already won. This is Zanshin.

Here we are using elements of Kendo practice to help instil the mind-set of attack

Fudoshin

There are four sicknesses of the mind that can stand between you and victory;

- Surprise
- Fear
- Doubt
- Perplexity

These sicknesses are not independent of each other, but are intertwined, leading in and out of each other constantly.

Something unforeseen can lead to surprise, doubt and then fear, fear freezes the body and can impair judgement, confusion and doubt can cause hesitation which can be fatal.

Fudoshin is our way of neutralising these sicknesses by training the mind, cultivating a mental determination that cannot be shaken or put off. This is the Imperturbable Spirit, or the Immoveable Mind.

Fudoshin. By Yasumoto Akiyoshi, Motoha Yoshin Ryu Soke

While this touches on the focus of Zanshin as previously discussed, Fudoshin is like a shield holding off anything that could shake you from your desired goal.

This toughness of the mind can be achieved through repeated training, performing Kata, or Waza while maintaining composure and keeping this idea firmly in your mind. There are no shortcuts, this takes time and repeated practice, but eventually it will become a natural zone you enter automatically when confronted.

Fudoshin is also our way of being unreadable to any opponent, like a poker face. No matter what happens during any encounter they must not see anything other than determination in your resolve, not even anger. Any emotional response will build your opponents confidence and encourage them so give them nothing. This should also be considered in training, by maintaining this composure at all times you can train yourself to the point where it is natural and happens without thought.

To fully understand Fudoshin therefore, we must also consider Mushin.

Fudoshin, being brushed by Akemi Lucas, Koshu Japanese Art, 2017

Mushin

The state of No Mind.

Not to be confused with mindlessness, the concept of No Mind is that of not allowing the mind to be taken or trapped by a single facet.

When this is achieved action can be instantaneous. The mind is not weighed down by all it is aware of, allowing the body to react naturally. Often people talk about having no hesitation, however this concept is much deeper than purely a lack of hesitation. Without Mushin the mind will consider the situation, and tell the body what to do. In this case even without any hesitation there is still delay while information is processed and a response decided.

Mushin by comparison removes this processing time, by not thinking and allowing the body to just react we can act instantly in any situation.

Think of when we hurt ourselves, step on something sharp or touch something hot, our bodies recoil and remove themselves from the situation before our mind has even grasped what has just happened. This is the state of mind we are striving for in our Jujutsu.

In his book Asayama Ichiden Ryu Taijutsu, Iwaki Hideo speaks of Meikyoshisui in terms of 'the Moon reflecting on the Water'

The water does not think about the moon as it holds its reflection, the effect is instant and achieved perfectly without thought.

If we look beneath the water we will no longer see the reflection, the water holds the reflection but does not absorb it, it cannot penetrate the surface. If from under the water we look to the moon however, we can still see it shining clearly in the sky.

This metaphor relates to our ability to see our opponent's actions, react instantly to them, while not allowing them to penetrate our spirit. In not allowing them to capture our thoughts or spirit, we cannot be tricked by them.

To take this a stage further, we can look at the actual word Meikyoshisui.

Meikyo (Shining Mirror)
Shishui (Still Water)

These words together describe how still water reflects perfectly like a shining mirror.

This is an important point, as the reflection is only perfect if the water is still, and the mirror shining. If the water is disturbed it will still reflect, but the effect is altered by ripples. If a mirror is dirty, it cannot reflect perfectly as it should, any mark on the mirror will become a part of the reflection.

In the same way, if we allow our opponent to disturb us, it will affect our judgement. If our minds are not as clear as the shining mirror, our thoughts will be contaminated and unable to work as intended. The sicknesses of the mind discussed before, surprise, fear, doubt, perplexity can all be thought of as disturbances in the water, or smudges on the mirror.

Fountain in Hagashi Honganji Temple, Kyoto

Metsuke

The meaning of this word is actually fairly simple, however as with the other concepts we have discussed, a simple translation can have many different contexts and different meanings.

目 Me (Eye)
付 Tsuke (Stick to, attach to)

There is a saying in Budo, 'Enzo no Metsuke' which refers to looking at your enemy how you would look at a distant mountain.

Often the bridge of the nose is discussed as the place where your gaze should settle, while also taking in the whole of the opponent's body, so that your focus isn't only on one specific spot.

In our practice however we focus very much on maintaining eye contact at all times. In doing this we can observe Uke's body and intentions, while also using our eyes to attack the mind-set of the opponent.

This to me is where Metsuke, Fudoshin and Zanshin walk hand in hand. Imagine taking all of the spirit and feeling we've discussed, the preparedness to fight, the confidence that you have already won, the total lack of fear of concern, and pushing that out through your gaze right into your opponent, along with a strong posture to destroy their resolve.

My daughter and another of my students in Southern England Yoshinkan Shibu Dojo - 2017

As you can see here, the effect of bringing these ideas together is formidable even in children. In this captured moment you can clearly see Zanshin, Fudoshin and Mushin coming together perfectly.

Uke's punch has been deflected, but he pays it no attention holding Tori's gaze unflinching and determined to continue, fully focused in the moment.

At the same time Tori has naturally moved in while deflecting Uke's attack, focused and holding their gaze, showing no concern over the attack, only a readiness and determination to fight.

Neither one shows any intention of backing down, they are both projecting confidence and determination through their eyes, with no concern over the small details. This is the kind of spirit that will see victory in a violent encounter.

Beauty in simplicity

In order to attain these states of mind, we must train our bodies in the postures, movement, and techniques required to the point where all becomes natural. We unconsciously step in the correct way, we don't need to think about the technique being applied to make it work.

This takes dedicated training, there are no shortcuts in this, everything must be practiced again and again, until the existing muscle programming of your body has been overwritten with the principles and techniques of your school.

For this to be possible in practice, we must also take away all unnecessary thought, and in many cases take away choice from a scenario.

If we have to think unnecessarily, or we have to make a choice, we are going back to the realm of consciousness, focused on ourselves or the opponent, and unable to react instantly.

To avoid this, we keep it simple. The less we have to think and decide, the better. To have any kind of chance, we must be able to act quickly and effectively.

The most effective schools are those that keep things simple. Often with only a limited number of very straight forward techniques which can be applied to any situation. This is also one of the biggest differences I see in western derived versions of Jujutsu, where over complicated and flashy techniques seem to be prevalent, and a 'more is better' approach to training.

If I can use one technique to react to anything an opponent throws at me, I no longer have to worry about how they will attack, or how I will respond, my mind will be free to focus on the whole situation and I will be able to respond naturally in the perfect instant, as discussed when talking of Mushin.

We see this even in competitive sport martial arts like Judo. With a large number of throws to choose from, matches are usually won with only a small number of core throws the Judoka can perform the best, and they have drilled and drilled and drilled. Or in Kendo, where matches are often decided with a single perfectly timed cut.

If we adopt the mind set of 'more is better' as mentioned above, we are really just learning a collection of techniques. The purity needed for real combat is diluted as soon as we plunge the mind back into having to consciously think of what to do, and therefore give the advantage to our opponent every time.

Keiko

Many practitioners of Japanese martial arts will be familiar with the term Keiko, but there is a deeper level to understanding this word and how it relates to our practice.

If we consider the word itself in more detail, Keiko;

稽   Think/Reflect

古   Old/Ancient

This gives us the idea of reflecting on the ancient, in this we begin to see how there is more to Keiko than just the physical act of training.

Breaking it down further, we can see that the character for Ko 古 is made up of two separate components;

十   Ten

口   Mouth

We can take the mouth to be a vessel for speaking and therefore consider it as a metaphor for passing on knowledge. The number 10 can then denote the idea of time, in this case 10 generations.

Looking back at the original word, rather than reflecting on the ancient, we can see now that we are reflecting on the knowledge transmitted over 10 generations, this is our connection to those who have gone before us.

We should all keep this in our minds when training, when practicing Kata for example it is not enough to just learn the movements and routine like some kind of dance, we should be considering the purpose of the Kata, the principles it was designed to teach us.

Many people who belong to Koryu feel very strongly about preserving their links to the past, including the Kata of their school, working tirelessly to ensure that they remain unchanged as passed down through generations.

In this word Keiko, I think we can practice freely, explore Henka to learn and grow more as individuals within the school, but always retain the connection to the past that is so important, the principles at the heart of the school and the lessons passed on for generations.

I feel this aspect is often overlooked in training, or even missing entirely, especially in modern forms of martial art, with focus being applied purely to the techniques being shown. You can see this clearly when schools have big flashy techniques that hold no relation to actual fighting, they have lost their connection to the past and while great feats of skill and impressive in demonstration, practicing in this way is not Keiko.

Kata

One of the most commonly used, and most effective ways of transmitting Japanese martial arts is through their Kata.

As a result of the huge popularity of Karate as well as Chinese martial arts, and heightened by countless movies in the 1980's, many people are familiar with the terms Kata and/or Form, but what generally springs to mind are solo sequences of various postures, blocks, and strikes usually seen performed by the hero before they go and save the day, win the tournament or whatever the case may be.

This remained my perception a long way into my own martial arts journey. Having practiced Chinese Martial Arts as a child, the concept of form was a familiar one, along with the understanding that kata was the Japanese counterpart. This was further emphasised within the modern form of Jujutsu I practiced, where included in its syllabus was a kata of blocks which had the familiar format of going through a sequence of choreographed movements alone.

The Kata practiced in Koryu Jujutsu, and some of the more modern systems that retain their links to the past however are quite different in practice.

While the overall purpose of the Kata is the same, to transmit the lessons of the school and facilitate the ability to train and practice these lessons safely, the way in which they are performed is different.

The Kata of Jujutsu are generally paired, with each partner taking on an important role in helping the other to learn. Attacks and counter techniques are then exchanged between the two in a specified manner to allow the key principles of the school, its methods and techniques, to be learned.

Basic structure

On the following pages are some examples of Jujutsu Kata, simply to provide an idea of the basic structure and how kata are performed.

Of course not all Kata will fit this model exactly, there will be differences between schools, and even branches of the same schools in how they perform Kata.

These examples have been taken from the Takagi Ryu, Omote no Kata (Also referred to as Shoden, or Shoden Omote in some branches)

As there are a number of branches of this school, each with their own slight variations on how they perform these kata, you may notice some differences compared to other sources available.

Kasumi Dori

1. Uke and Tori create the correct Maai and take Kiza no Kamae

2. Uke steps forward and performs attack, gripping Tori's lapel

3. Tori counters with Shuto

Kasumi Dori

4. Tori continues with Gyaku Waza and takes Uke into a control position, along with a kick to Uke's side

5. Tori safely disengages, maintaining Zanshin

Do Gaeshi

1. Uke and Tori create the correct Maai and take Kiza no Kamae

2. Tori steps forward and performs attack

3. Tori takes Uke to the ground

4. Tori flips Uke face down into a control position

5. Tori safely disengages, maintaining Zanshin

Kata Mune Dori

1. Tori steps forward to apply pressure while creating the correct Maai

2. Uke attacks

3. Tori begins to apply Kuzushi

4. Tori applies Kuzushi and brings Uke into vulnerable position

5. Tori throws Uke to the floor, maintaining Zanshin

You can see that the general structure of these Kata are all similar. They resemble potential fighting scenarios, practiced in a controlled manner.

I say resemble, as a common mistake that I often see when people learn and practice Kata is to believe that the they are supposed to replicate 'real' fighting, when in fact this is not the case.

Kata are designed to transmit key fighting principles and techniques, along with a number of other things I will cover in this book, but at no time should they be considered the same as actual fighting.

Another mistake I see, is to think in terms of 'this technique for that attack' rather than as mentioned when discussing Keiko, reflecting on what the Kata is intended to teach. The danger here, is that in reality, things don't go to plan, attacks don't come exactly as they do when training, if you focus on a specific technique for a specific attack, you will not be able to cope when something different or new happens.

Kata have to be systemised in a way that will allow the techniques and principles of the school to be passed along. So when someone attacks you in Kata, and you respond as the Kata dictates, initially you will understand it as a specific defence for the attack given, but the intention is that your understanding of this will move beyond these limits through your own Keiko.

Unfortunately I've seen many 'highly ranked' black belts who have never made it beyond this point, usually the idea of 'the more the better' previously discussed is more appealing than true consolidation of the core system and principles. The result being endless variations of techniques that have no basis in reality, created in the purely safe environment of the Dojo, and while impressive to watch, most are reliant on Uke standing completely still and are therefore absolutely useless in any type of fighting situation.

Application of Kata and Henka

It is easy to understand why people may think that individual Kata are simply designed to teach you what to do if someone throws a particular attack, like mentioned previously. That is precisely what it looks like when you see anyone demonstrating Kata.

Now while that is certainly a part of what is being taught, if you fixate on this point alone you may miss the other lessons available in the kata, and the intended application of the techniques.

Think of a lapel grab for example, why would someone grab you in this way? Are they intending to pull you onto a knife thrust? Are they going to shove you backwards? Are they attempting to hold your jacket closed so you can't reach for a weapon? Even though in kata this may be represented by a simple hold, you can see already any number of possibilities that this attack could represent.

In one of the kata examples, Tori responded to this type of attack with instant Atemi, before Uke had any chance to consolidate their position or continue with their attack. In doing this you can see that if considered properly, this response is capable of tackling any of the potential variations in the purpose of the attack mentioned previously.

Again however, if we fixate on that point alone, we can easily miss the fact that this principle of instantaneous Atemi can also apply to many other situations, not just someone grabbing your lapel. Thinking of the offensive strategy I mentioned earlier, if the timing of the strike was changed you can even prevent Uke from ever taking a grip on your collar.

When this is understood we can start to see the real purpose of the Kata more clearly, you are being taught a key fighting principle that you can apply in **any** situation.

Now already we begin to see a world being opened up in front of us in the form of Kata, but in truth we have just scratched the surface looking at the first movement. The basic movements of most Kata can actually be learned in just a matter of moments, the effective use and understanding of the principles being transmitted however can take a lifetime to really master.

That is the beauty of Kata, and in this way we are really undertaking Keiko.

I see a number of instructors who advertise separate 'Combative' or 'Self Defence' training, based on the kata of whatever Jujutsu system they practice.

Where I see this happening, it usually suggests to me that those teaching are ignorant of the real purpose of Kata and how it fits within Keiko, and are simply performing the Kata of the school without really understanding them.

An effective system of Jujutsu needs no separate combat training, it is (or should be) combative in nature already and the instructor should be able to convey this understanding to their students.

This type of thing also boosts the perception held by some that traditional Martial Arts are not effective in the modern world. In fact this suggests to me that the instructors in question do not fully believe in their own systems and therefore have to compensate with their 'combative' training.

I fully, and honestly, believe that Jujutsu if taught properly, and trained with the correct spirit, is a completely efficient and effective method of fighting, and that is how I approach every Keiko.

The author teaching Takagi Ryu Kata at the Kodosai Japanese Cultural Event, 2013

Reiho (Methods of bowing)

Martial arts training can have a strong psychological effect on us, especially when training with true Zanshin and the feeling of real threat and violence. When this type of training is pushed to extreme levels, focusing on destroying an opponent and fighting with no pause, you can see how easily we may fall into a state of primitive aggression, possibly without even realising it.

Our shield against this, is to maintain correct etiquette at all times. Everything begins and ends with Reiho for this very reason.

'any martial style without this in its teachings is simply training fighting animals and not a spiritual path for humans'
- Tanemura Shoto, KJJR Jujutsu Volume 1

There are numerous ways in which to bow to your partner, depending on circumstance. Whether standing, kneeling, with or without a weapon, for duelling, higher or lower status, clothing, etc. These will also vary from school to school, over the page are some examples.

Ritsu Rei

Seiza Rei

Koshiki Rei

Kamae

Kamae is a term used to describe the stances or postures a practitioner will use when performing techniques or Kata. These will vary from school to school. Some having many, others only one or two. Some will have the feel of a fighting stance, such as found in karate or even boxing, while others prefer more natural Kamae, as if you were just standing or walking along.

As well as these type of Kamae, there are also Kamae or positions that you may enter in the process of performing a technique, or evading an attack.

To think of Kamae only in these terms however is incorrect and not a true representation of how important posture is to Budo.

The use of Kamae, especially when incorporating Metsuke, Zanshin, Fudoshin and some of the things we will discuss shortly, is a very powerful tool in the arsenal of a Budoka. The right Kamae can put fear into your opponent, can trick them, provoke them into making a mistake, control their movement while at the same allowing you to move freely and quickly with devastating effect.

Chuden no Kamae   Zanshin no Kamae

By comparing one of our Jujutsu Kamae here with one found in various Kenjutsu Ryu, you can see a number of similarities, highlighting some of the points discussed earlier in the book about the origin of these Kamae.

Notice the slight bend in the legs, and raised rear heel, not too much but waiting there like a coiled spring, allowing sudden and instantaneous movement both in and out as required. Allowing you to take full advantage of any opportunity presented to you by quickly springing forward and cutting or striking alike.

Also note the proximity of the feet when looking head on, and the square angle of the hips. Look at the placement of your own feet when you walk or run, your feet will usually pass by each other very closely, and you will move in the direction your hips are facing. These Kamae are taking full advantage of these natural principles of movement.

Shizen no Kamae

Here is an interesting Kamae, that I feel many people misunderstand.

Similar to Zanshin no Kamae, except for the placement of the feet. Notice as before the proximity of the feet when looking head on, they are close together again, but this time they are side by side.

This Kamae as before is utilising the natural principle of movement, but taking it a step further. If you watch your feet as you walk, at the beginning and end of your steps your feet are just as they were in Zanshin no Kamae, whereas at mid step they are side by side just as they are here. This can represent being attacked while walking, rather than being considered as a fighting stance.

This is why I say I feel people misunderstand this particular Kamae. I often see people practicing techniques and standing with the legs spread out, at shoulder width or even wider. While this may provide a potentially stronger base, when you consider the aspects of walking and circumstance of attack this makes no sense.

A very deceptive Kamae here, similar to Seiza. This Kamae gives the impression of having limited movement and that of being fixed in place.

As opposed to Seiza however, where the feet are resting on the insteps, in this fighting Kamae the feet rest on their balls with the toes flexed.

This allows easier movement, standing up, or by lifting either knee an ability to shift very quickly off the centre line while maintaining perfect balance.

Kiza no Kamae

There is also another practical reason for using this Kamae in Jujutsu training, and that is to avoid moving on 'dead feet,' where the feet rest on the instep as in Seiza. There is a high risk of injury if weight is placed on the foot in a way that overextends the tendons. This is why when rising from Seiza it is correct to first raise onto the balls of the feet before any weight is placed.

Kuzushi

This is another word commonly used, but I feel not fully understood in Japanese martial arts.

Most people you ask, including instructors will quickly be able to tell you that Kuzushi is breaking the balance of your opponent, and then go on to inform you of its importance when executing throws.

Now it's important to understand that this is not wrong. As a description of Kuzushi, and how it can apply to martial arts, it is correct. However, it is also in my opinion a biased description that doesn't give the whole picture. This idea has possibly come about as a result of the popularity of Judo and the fact that this definition applies perfectly to a sport focused predominantly on throwing.

If we look at the word itself outside of a Martial Arts context, and the related verbs;

Kuzusu / Kuzureru (崩す) which can have the following definitions;
- To collapse, to crumble
- To get out of shape, to lose ones shape, to become disorganised, to become untidy
- To break down, to be thrown into disarray
- To destroy, to demolish, to pull down, to tear down, to level
- To disturb, to put into disorder, to throw off balance, to make shaky

We can see here a destructive theme throughout, breaking down, losing shape, demolition, an example when used in conversation could be referring to demolishing a house, or levelling a structure.

While throwing off balance is an element, it is clearly not the whole.

When applying Kuzushi we are not simply breaking balance, we are breaking down Uke's structure first and foremost, disrupting their centre or occupying it, to create a situation where they are unable to continue their attack, and we can gain control. This will often facilitate a position where throwing is possible and balance is broken, however that is not always the ultimate goal.

To explain further, here are some examples;

Mae (Front)

Shown in these pictures are a selection of grabs and strikes from the front.

With any attack from the front, no matter the target, a simple truth is that your opponent must move toward you.

This is an important fact when considering structure. To move toward you and attack, Uke's posture will have to allow them to freely move forward, they will be moving toward you as they attack so will have to be stepping.

As you can see here in each case, Uke's leg is forward, highlighting this fact of movement.

Here Uke's right leg is forward in each case, this is purely for ease in explaining structure, the actual foot forward is not important here.

Another important point is the straightness of the back and the position of the hips shown in the pictures.

Consider when you walk or run, your hips have to be forward, and square, otherwise you have a really hard time moving.

A real danger point with these type of attacks (often overlooked as many train techniques from purely static positions) is the mass and momentum of Uke themselves, in each example their entire mass is heading for you. If not dealt with, even if you avoid being hit, or you have a fantastic technique to deal with being grabbed, you can be easily run down by them in this way. This is why I have placed so much focus here on the breaking of structure to prevent a continued attack.

Let's now look at some ways in which we can apply Kuzushi to these attacks, and disrupt Uke's structure;

In this example, Tori is using contact and pressure on Uke's arm not only to deflect the punch, but as you can see in the picture, to turn Uke's body and in turn their hips.

Uke's hips are now pointing offline to Tori's right hand side, in this position they cannot physically move toward Tori without a readjustment, so if they continue their attack they will go past rather than collide. Giving a split second respite in which Tori can act.

You can also see that this effect on Uke's structure is exaggerated further as the pressure is being applied toward a point that intersects with the direction the hips are now facing, with some downward pressure also applied.

The turning of the hips while in motion has created a situation where Uke has stepped one way, but their hips are now pointing in a different direction. In this position, any pressure applied in the direction of the hips (either forwards or backwards) cannot be resisted as there is no stabilising leg to support the body, creating an over extended structure, allowing techniques to be applied. Tori however has maintained his position and now controls Uke's centre.

Here Tori is using the same principle as in the previous example to break Uke's attacking structure, deflecting mass in the same direction and exploiting the same weakness in the created structure.

The difference here however, is that Tori is using Uke's grip as the contact point rather than the push seen before, and as such this is lower on the body than a punch to the face. As the wrist is almost at the same level as the hips, by creating the turn their position is already adequate for creating the overextended position desired.

In this example Kuzushi is being applied in the opposite direction. As shown in the picture by applying pressure to Uke's right hand side, and in turn shifting their upper body in that direction, the structure of the attack is broken. Uke's upper body is now out of line with the hips and overextended, again making it difficult to continue the attack without a readjustment, and beginning to off balance in that direction.

The author practicing Kuzushi with Salur Onural, Dojo-shu of Tokueikan Dojo, 2016

Ushiro (Behind)

Here are some examples of attacks from behind.*

Looking at the top picture, Uke is attacking from behind by gripping Tori tightly around the arms.

The purpose of this attack would likely be one of the following;

- To pull backwards and/or down to the floor
- To lift and throw
- To restrain

The bottom picture is very similar, although rather than gripping around the arms, Uke is attempting to apply a choke.

Notice in either case, Uke is very close. To exert any control over Tori at all, he must be. Not just close in fact, but there must be bodily contact.

This point becomes even clearer when looking at the potential purposes of this attack listed above. In any of those cases, the arms alone are just not physically strong enough to exert the power needed, even with the largest, strongest of people. The arms and body must work together and combine the strength of the whole body.

*For the purpose of looking at structure here, I have used simple attacks from behind that involve contact. Other types of attack, struck as being hit from behind are very difficult to predict, and fall into different discussions around situational awareness, or sixth sense type of abilities some claim to have. As a pragmatist, I would prefer to deal with what I can see or feel.

This means that without even having to look, we can be sure of certain things in these types of attack;

- Uke must be square to you
  If they are side on they will not be able to exert the control needed.

- Uke's hips will be forward.
  If you follow normal health and safety advice for lifting, the advice is to lift with the legs, holding whatever you are lifting close to the body with your back straight. This is no different, to keep your back straight your hips must be square and forward.

- Uke's grip will be pulling you backwards, toward themselves.

I've seen many examples where people practice without this bodily contact, which I will discuss further when looking at Ukemi but for now, it is enough to understand that any attack will not be effective without these points, which is important as we now look at some ways in which we can apply Kuzushi.

As we know that for an effective attack Uke's hips must be forward and square, while also very close, we can use this point to apply Kuzushi.

As shown in the picture simply by using our own hips to strike Uke's, we can compromise their structure and take any power out of their attack, we can also add to this effect by stretching out their arms and beginning to off balance them. This structure break is only momentary through, it only takes a slight adjustment on Uke's part for them to be back to strength, so any response must be instant, like the throw depicted here.

In this picture however, we are going the opposite way, and stepping forward, in turn extending Uke's arms and bringing their upper body forward. Again, for only a split second this creates an angle in Uke's structure where their body is further forward than their hips, taking away stability and power, while also breaking the bodily contact reducing their control and allowing room to move.

By applying Atemi at the same time this effect can be greatly exaggerated, as shown here with the elbow.

It is important in this case to act before they have managed to gain a good grip, and have begun to pull you back. If you try this method while being pulled backwards you will be fighting against Uke's strength and will no longer be practicing Jujutsu.

If Uke is fast and has already begun to pull you back, you can assist their movement by applying energy while deflecting the pull. By turning the body here and lifting the arm in time with Uke's pull. Their arm will side up the top of your arm, breaking their structure and again creating a posture where their body is forward of their hips.

Real Kuzushi lies in breaking down your opponent's structure to create a state where they are unable to continue their attack. The hips are the real secret to this, when the feet aren't in line with the hips, or the body is overextended it is very difficult to move and/or resist any balance break.

Examples of kuzushi, showing that size is not important when breaking structure

Timing

This was touched on slightly previously when looking at kuzushi, but here I will discuss in a little more detail.

One of the most important points to consider when applying kuzushi is the timing, in fact it is essential for any kind of effective result.

This is not to say that you must get a specific timing correct every time, as this would be an unobtainable goal. When talking about real life fighting situations things can happen extremely fast, things can go wrong, attacks may be unorthodox, any number of factors could affect what happens.

We saw an example of this when looking at the attacks from behind, where the response changed slightly dependant on whether Uke was in the process of gripping, or pulling back. As we saw then this can impact the effectiveness of any technique you try to apply.

If you move forward while they are pulling you back, you fight against their strength, if you move back while they are entering to grab you, you fight against their strength, the skill is in recognising the movement and reacting in an appropriate manner. This is Jujutsu.

To look at an example let's consider men tsuki (punch to the face)

Uke steps forward and delivers a punch, we looked earlier at applying kuzushi to carry the attack past and overextend their centre past their hips.

Now if we consider Uke's bodyweight, while they are delivering the punch and stepping forward their weight is moving rapidly forward. This movement is unrestricted as one foot is off the ground. At the end of the movement however when the foot has landed, Uke's weight is then grounded and they are harder to redirect.

The optimum timing therefore when dealing with this type of attack is while Uke is still in motion.

As we saw in the pictures of this type of attack, kuzushi may still be applied once the foot has planted, we just need to be aware that this is the case and adapt as necessary.

Tori – Uke relationship / Ukemi

Over the past few pages we have been focused on structure, and the breaking of it. We continue this now when looking at the role of Uke and their relationship with Tori.

Something I have seen time and time again is training where the Uke is nothing more than a punch bag, or throwing dummy, getting pummelled by Tori, just waiting for their turn to get up and have their turn. Now, while this type of training can be fun, especially when you are younger, it doesn't fulfil the role Uke should be playing.

Although the meaning of the word Ukemi is receiving body, this doesn't mean that all Uke is supposed to do is take whatever Tori throws at them. Uke's primary role is to help Tori to learn.

It does Tori no good at all if during Keiko Uke just falls like a rag doll at every movement. Tori doesn't get to learn what really worked and what didn't, and can build a false sense of their own ability if ever tested for real.

Likewise, it would do them no good to make movement awkward through tensing and resisting. This changes the dynamic of the technique and Tori has to fight you instead of learning how to apply the technique correctly.

It is important therefore, that Uke attacks with good structure, strong hips, forward and in line with the feet, with their back straight, and attempts to maintain that structure throughout, but holding it naturally without resistance.

The author taking Ukemi for Andy McCormack, Motoha Yoshin Ryu British Sohonbu-Cho, 2016

In this way, Tori can see and feel what is happening clearly, they can learn how to truly apply Kuzushi and make techniques work properly. If Kuzushi hasn't been applied in the right way, Uke will stay put, if it has, they will fall, or whatever the case may be.

In certain cases resistance can be built as Tori progresses, but a fact I find interesting (especially when watching some clubs training with huge amounts of resistance) is that the resistance applied is often fake and absolutely useless for training.

To clarify this point, the resistance is applied only because the training situation makes it possible, and the training situation is one of safety, learning, and as mentioned previously not necessarily a true reflection of a fighting scenario.

A good example of this is the wristlock Kote Gaeshi. It is very easy for Uke to resist this throw, by simply tensing up the arm and also taking a small step back, the angles are changed, Kuzushi is broken and the technique can be resisted...... all makes sense, yes?

But then consider the timing I spoke about earlier. If Uke is caught mid-step, Kuzushi applied and the technique carried out instantaneously, all of this will happen as their arm is travelling forward in a punch and the foot is off the ground.

Is this instance it is impossible to step back or correct the hips, as Uke is in mid-step. It is impossible to tense the arm to resist as it is being thrown as a punch, you can't physically move in this way and tense at the same time, hence this type of resistance being fake.

Uke should always be mindful of these points, and create the best learning environment for Tori.

The role of Uke doesn't stop there though, not by a long shot...

All training is training, especially in the case of taking the role of Uke, there is no downtime.

An important aspect of training for Uke is in the practice of attacks, whether punching someone in the face, pinning their wrist so they can't draw a weapon, wrestling them to the ground from behind, or any number of other offensive movements.

It is no good to perform half-hearted attacks, this does Tori no good as they don't have the best attacks to learn from, but it is also no good for Uke as they are not training properly.

Earlier in the book I mentioned offensive action, pre-emptive attack, and the importance of this in real fighting.

When practicing Kata, Tori knows which attack you will be giving them, and how to respond safely, which gives Uke the opportunity to choose their timing, and when ready launch a true attack on target and with full spirit, while maintaining a safe training environment.

This again highlights the importance of the relationship between Uke and Tori.

A further purpose of Ukemi, as the name would suggest is actually learning how to receive techniques without injury.

This is another important point. Unless you are watching a movie, where the hero destroys an entire army without taking a single blow themselves, the likelihood in a real fight is that someone will do something to you. By training continuously the receiving of techniques, you will learn to feel what's happening long before you see it and will be able to adapt to ensure minimum impact.

Taking this a step further, once you understand how to safely receive a technique to the level where you can feel it, you will also be able to escape easily and even counter.

Dojo Training 2017

Nagashi / Nagare

The words Nagashi or Nagare translate as flow. If you consider the actual Kanji for this word 流 you may notice that it is the same character as used for the word 'Ryu' which also translates as flow, and the character actually resembles a waterfall.

The context in which it is used is quite different however.

When talking of Ryu in the context of schools (Takagi Ryu, Motoha Yoshin Ryu, Takenouchi Ryu, for example) the reference to flow relates to knowledge being transmitted from teacher to student in a continuous flow.

When we talk of Nagashi however, we are talking about the actual physical act of flowing. Making techniques flow just like the water of a river, never stopping even when hurdles are met, just change course and carry on, and once momentum is built even flow straight over or through an obstacle.

There are a number of benefits of this;

Without Nagashi techniques have a stop-start feel that will make Kata, and then fighting clunky and ineffective.

When applying Kuzushi this stop-start approach will prevent you from being able to easily manipulate Uke's position, as their weight will plant during any breaks in motion, and they will have the chance to resist.

When momentum is broken, additional energy is required to start the movement again, this applies to any stops made during a technique and any advantage will be lost.

We also have to understand that when fighting there will certainly be hurdles, an opponent can change suddenly, a technique may not work, you may be surprised. In any of these scenarios, if you stop or hesitate even for a fraction of a second, you will lose any advantage and be on the back foot.

We must be ready to flow at any instant, we meet a hurdle so we change and flow into something else, if that doesn't work, something else, and so on until we succeed. This is a physical manifestation of the mental attitudes discussed earlier.

Nagashi is a word often heard from Yasumoto Sensei in training, and an important factor in Motoha Yoshin Ryu, with Kata designed to transmit this exact point.

Maai (Fighting Distance)

Maai is the word used to describe the empty space between Uke and Tori when practicing Kata or techniques, however a more accurate way to look at this when talking of martial arts would be to consider the distance and time between the two.

This dictates how quickly an attack can be delivered, the type of attack possible and the potential threat level of your position. Learning how to assess and manipulate it therefore is a very important aspect of training.

Through subtle body movements it is possible to remove yourself from an opponent's striking range without them noticing, or even move into striking distance ready to attack while they still feel safe. We can therefore look at it as the deliberate space between.

While we are talking about distance, it is not possible to classify this into actual measurements. Too many factors can alter the Maai, larger or smaller opponents, whether weapons are involved, a sword has a longer reach than a punch for example, Bo even more, Yari longer still. The Maai for each of these being different to the others.

Maai can be broken down into different levels, regardless of the variations listed above. I have explained some of these in the context of Jujutsu.

Toi Maai (distant interval)

This is where Uke cannot reach you and deliver their attack with a single movement. At this Maai the threat level is fairly low as Uke would have to cross the distance to attack, giving you warning.

The same is also true of Tori however, making any pre-emptive action difficult.

Issoku Maai (one step interval)

As the name would suggest, this is where Uke can deliver their attack within the space of one movement. This is the most common Maai to attack from when practicing Jujutsu Kata.

The threat level here is higher, as you can be attacked suddenly without warning with less time to respond.

Tori can also reach Uke within the same amount of time, pre-emptive attack becomes a more viable option in this position.

Chikai maai (close interval)

This Maai is different to the other two, in that certain attacks can be hindered by closeness. In order to attack properly either Uke or Tori would need to move backwards creating space.

When in this Maai the danger from standard strikes can be less, however the threat level of this Kamae remains high, as grappling, throwing, restraining, close quarter strikes such as head-butt's are still possible with no forewarning.

In Jujutsu, we often enter this Maai in order to manipulate Uke's structure while also making it difficult for them to continue attacking.

Waza

While Kata transmit the ideas, strategies and principles of a school, the Waza are at the core of this. The actual techniques of the school.

These can generally be broken down into the following types

Atemi Waza – Striking Technique
Gyaku Waza – Joint locking and reversal Technique
Nage Waza – Throwing Technique
Shime Waza – Strangle & choking Technique

The ways in which these are used and applied will vary from school to school, as well as the level of focus applied to each.

If you watch martial arts footage available online through websites like Youtube, it will not usually be long before you see some very fancy and complicated looking techniques. These techniques can be interesting to watch, and are often performed well and show the effort and training that has been put in.

Many people see these complicated combinations and consider them to be advanced level, and something to aspire to, but in truth the opposite is very much the case when looking for techniques that will work in the case of real violence.

Complicated techniques simply don't work in real fighting. When someone tries to take your head off with a punch, they aren't usually inclined to stand still afterwards and allow a flurry of strikes to be performed, or for you to get the right grip to perform your technique, and any friends they have with them wont usually stand around idly while you tie your opponent up in knots on the floor.

It is easy to become carried away while in dojo with a compliant partner, with all of the different possibilities and manipulations that can be applied to the human body to cause pain, to throw, to put combinations together, but none of this has anything to do with actual fighting and only serves to dilute the system you are practicing.

I'm aware that this may sound very flippant and some may take offense at this point of view, however time and time again this is exactly what I see being taught.

In my opinion the techniques of authentic Jujutsu and their application should always be simple. This is what you will usually find in authentic Koryu, especially those founded earlier in history.

Atemi Waza

While the striking of Jujutsu is not the same as found in some other martial arts, it is important to note that strikes are an integral part of the system. Probably the purest form of technique, the fastest, and often the most effective way to neutralise a threat, strikes are a key aspect in the strategy of Jujutsu.

This is under-played in many schools, with strikes taking a back seat and seen only as an aid to the grappling techniques. I've seen examples where strikes have been removed almost entirely, or are performed half-heartedly, right through to examples where there is a completely over exaggerated expectation of what a particular strike will do in a given situation.

'Hit them here to knock them out' or 'strike here to break their collar bone' or similar examples I know you will all have heard before. I'm sure I've said the same kind of things myself when teaching in the past.

The trouble with this comes in when no training is actually undertaken in regard to striking. Without repeated training, any strike is practically useless and likely to cause you more harm than your opponent.

Consider boxers for a moment, these are some of the most physically powerful, hard hitting people in the world. They spend hours upon hours learning and training the best methods to punch, and conditioning their hands, the ultimate goal to achieve a knock out win in the ring. If you watch boxing matches, it is very rare for someone to be knocked out cleanly with one punch, even a few punches. A knock out win has usually been built up and prepped through repeated strikes, weakening the opponent, head shots, kidney shots, stomach shots, ending with the coveted knock out blow.

Even then, while the boxer throwing the punches knows that they have the power and form to deliver a 'knock out' blow, it is not as simple as that. The target is moving and even a landed punch can deflect depending on where it hits, the human body itself is very tough when it wants to be, and it doesn't want to be knocked out. All of these things must be trained for if a boxer wishes to be successful.

Now, if this is what we see when watching professional boxers fighting, how can we ever expect to achieve these type of results without practicing strikes at all? The rest of our Jujutsu repertoire will be difficult to execute if we break our hand with an initial strike.

Now some may argue that striking is included in Kata, or in certain techniques, so they are training it.

In truth, while that type of training is great for learning strategy, for developing form, fluidity, and speed. It is not doing anything to prepare your hand for the impact of a strike, to develop the actual power needed to deliver a knock out punch, or a bone breaking Shuto.

If you look at different martial arts, or within Jujutsu specifically look at different schools, you will see any number of ways in which to strike with the hands, how to form a fist, how to deliver a blow, etc.

Any part of the body can also be used to deliver Atemi, the head, feet, knees, elbows, fingers...

Rather than go into each of these, I will detail here just a few basic strikes that I am familiar with and believe to be effective;

Kobushi Ate

As the name suggests, this is an old style fist.

While this looks similar to the Ippon Ken used in some other arts, it is not the same and should not be confused.

This fist comes directly from the Te no Uchi (hand technique) of Kenjutsu, used when holding the sword.

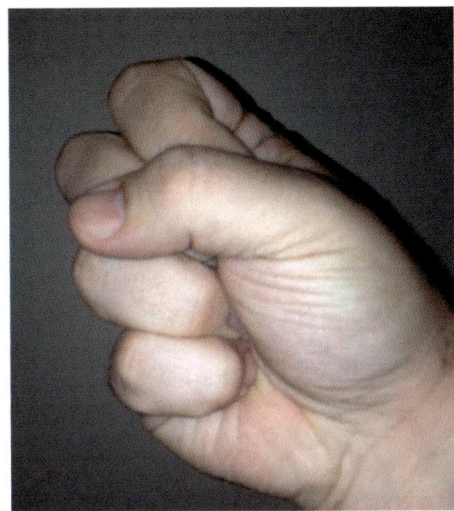

The last two fingers gripping tightly, while the middle finger, fore finger and thumb remain relaxed.

This results in a slightly twisted fist, with the middle knuckle protruding, intended to strike vulnerable points.

The slightly relaxed fingers, when held in this way give a certain level of protection against impact, but the structure prevents the fist from collapsing when a strike is delivered.

This fist can be thrown in a number of ways, however I believe the most effective to be direct, along a straight line and with no initial change in position or telegraphing. So if your hand is at your side, the strike is delivered in a straight line from there, if your hands are up, thrown straight from that point at your desired target. Any adjustment to your hand position in readying yourself to strike can be observed by your opponent, so you should avoid this.

The main areas I target with this type of strike are Jinchu (the area just below the septum, and above the teeth) or suigetsu (the base of the sternum)

With this type of fist, a large amount of damage can be caused by striking these areas, however as previously discussed this is not guaranteed, we should continue any attack as if the opponent is still able to fight. Hesitation here could mean defeat, even after you have delivered the blow.

I have seen this happen many times in real life. Someone delivers a substantial blow and then stops, expecting the opponent to be knocked unconscious. But in that moment, the opponent comes back with a strike of their own and takes the advantage and wins.

Shuto

The Shuto Uchi (knife hand strike) is a very fast and effective type of Atemi.

It can be thrown horizontally, vertically or diagonally, mirroring any of the potential cutting directions of the sword.

The fingers are held together, and bent to an angle of around 45 degrees. This bend strengthens the hand, enabling it to endure extra hard striking, and strikes to harder areas of the body, avoiding the injuries a straight hand or a fist may be subject to.

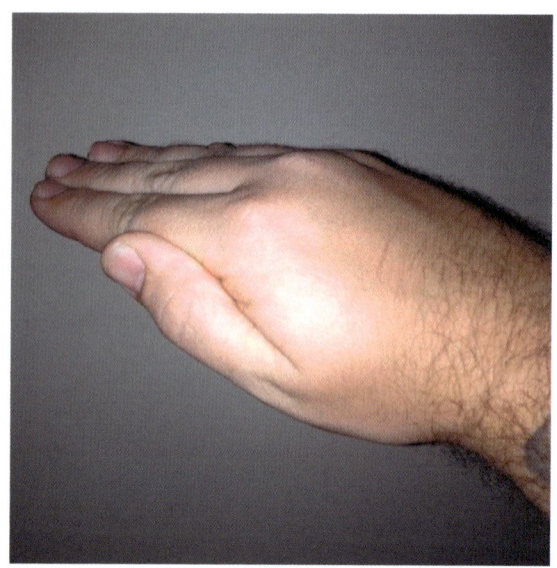

As this strike can attack to the sides of Uke, vulnerable points like the temple, neck, or the ribs are exposed. The collar bone, or shoulder and neck muscles are also in danger from vertical, or diagonal strikes.

I have seen in some schools these strikes delivered from above the head, or in large arc like movements. As with Kobushi Ate I always perform these strikes directly, shooting them straight at the target without no telegraphing. I believe this is an important point when performing Atemi in Jujutsu, strikes should be explosive, sudden, fast, and committed, removing wherever possible your opponents chance to counter.

Shuto Uchi can also be referred to as Nukiuchi in some scenarios.

Taken from Iaijutsu's Nukitsuke, the Shuto here resembles the movement of drawing a sword straight into a cut, with the strike delivered along the same cutting line, the edge of the hand replacing the sharp edge of the sword.

The throat is a likely target for this type of attack, with the strike being delivered in a straight line as above.

Dojo Training 2016

Gyaku Waza

A real trademark of Jujutsu, and a major area of strength lies in the joint locking and reversal techniques.

These can be extremely painful and destructive when applied, allowing the practitioner the ability to control and arrest an opponent, generate a specific movement in response, or to break, shatter or dislocate joints.

In my opinion, because it is very impressive within a dojo, and when showing others the techniques of Jujutsu, too much attention is placed on causing pain through the application of joint locks, which highlights a lack of understanding of real fighting that can be dangerous.

Once an opponent has been brought under control, a painful restraint can be effective to prevent struggle or attempts to escape. Until this point however, the opponent poses a threat that must be neutralised. Neutralising the opponent is far more important at this stage than causing pain, if we fixate purely on causing pain, it is easy to come completely unstuck very quickly when things don't go our way.

Full of adrenaline the opponent may not even feel the pain you are trying to apply, or may be able to resist it. Even if they can't resist indefinitely ask yourself 'how many times can they hit me with their other hand while I try to make this technique work?' In these scenarios joint locks should be applied to affect the body structure of the opponent, to prevent further attack, or to destroy the joint completely, disabling their ability to attack.

While pain will always be a factor in doing this (I can't imagine a dislocated elbow ever being described as painless) it should not be the main point of focus. Many techniques can be applied in ways which are very painful in the dojo, but are of little to no use outside of a compliant training relationship. To avoid performing these kind of techniques we should always keep in mind the desired result of the technique, not the pain that can be generated.

While there are many variations on how joint locking may be performed, many different types of manipulation as well as the many joints in the human body and how they can be attacked, they generally fall into 3 main categories; Hyper Extension, Compression, and Rotation, and consist of either moving a joint in a way that it is not meant to bend, or by overextending the natural movement of the joint.

I will explain here in more detail;

Hyper Extension

In this method a hinge joint such as the elbow is extended beyond its full range.

As shown in the picture here, the arm is held straight, the shoulder and wrist are in fixed positions, in this state any pressure applied to the elbow will cause it to over extend.

This can be very painful as a restraint, or can be used to dislocate the elbow completely with relative ease.

This method can be applied to any hinge joint found within the body, elbows, knees, even fingers.

Dojo training, Yonago, Japan, 2017

Compression

This method involves taking an ellipsoidal joint such as the wrist and moving it outside or beyond its normal range of movement by compressing it.

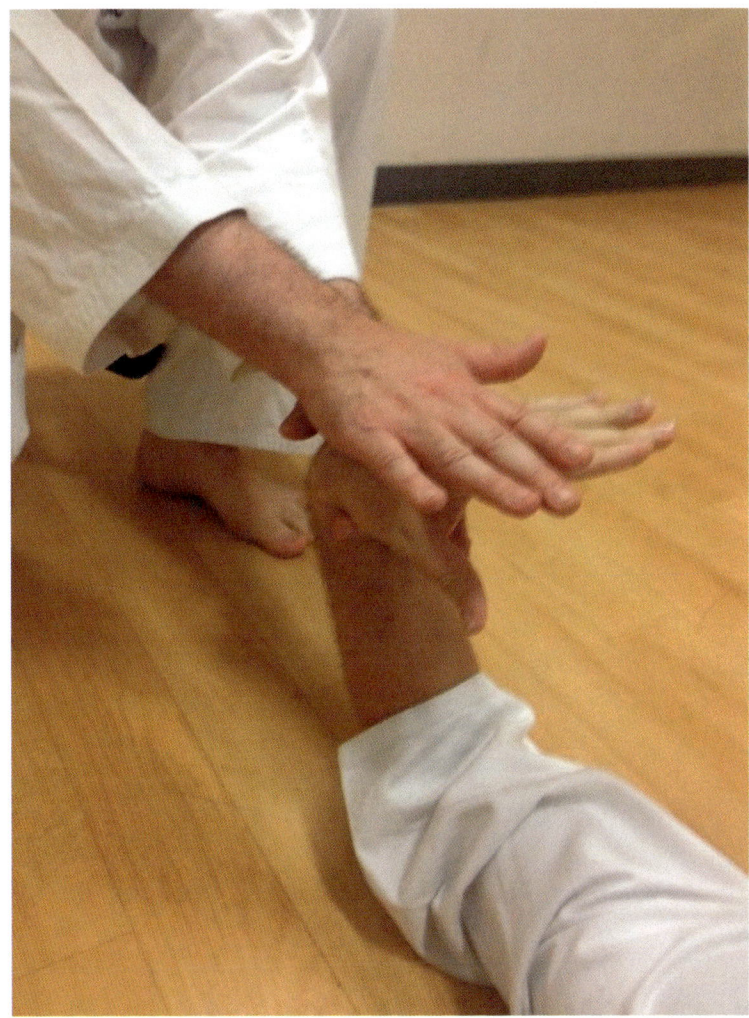

This can be done by running the joint along its usual course and continuing beyond the usual stopping place, or by applying pressure in an alternate direction where movement is more limited.

Rotation

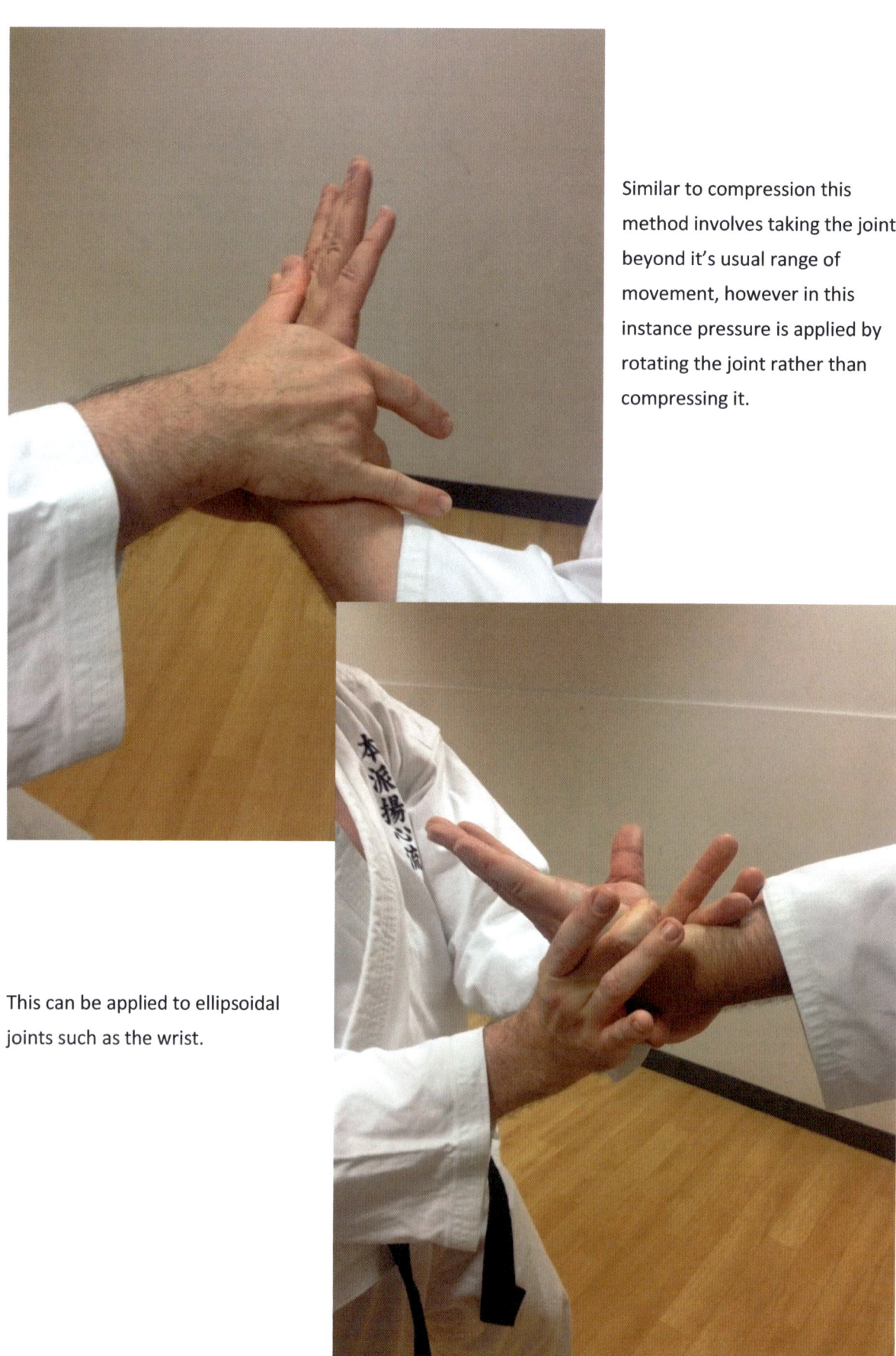

Similar to compression this method involves taking the joint beyond it's usual range of movement, however in this instance pressure is applied by rotating the joint rather than compressing it.

This can be applied to ellipsoidal joints such as the wrist.

Nage Waza

For ease here, I am going to define throwing techniques as anything that involves taking an opponent from a standing position to the ground.

There are different forms of Nage Waza, generally falling into the categories discussed on the next few pages, with many throws in fact falling into multiple categories.

The author teaching Nage Waza. 2016

Kuzushi

An important point underpinning them all is Kuzushi, as discussed earlier in this book. Without this throwing becomes a very difficult task. If an opponent can maintain their posture and structure, they are strong, can catch their balance easily and move around.

It is essential therefore to break down their structure and prevent their ability to regain their composure to allow easy throwing.

Some throws however are possible purely as a result of creating Kuzushi, without the need of any of the other examples listed on the next few pages.

Lifting and throwing the opponent to the ground

In these techniques the opponent is physically picked up and thrown to the ground, using body mechanics to create a situation where they become weightless and can be lifted easily onto the hip, shoulder(s) or other part of the body dependant on the particular throw being performed.

Using a joint lock to throw the opponent to the ground

With these techniques the opponent's joints are manipulated to cause pain and create Kuzushi, and in turn a situation where the continuation of the movement throws them down.

Sweeping or trapping the opponent's legs

These throws are performed by preventing the opponent from being able to take a step to catch their balance by blocking their leg, sweeping their leg away entirely with your own leg, or other part of the body or knocking it away in more of a striking method.

Using the opponent's own momentum

These techniques involve intercepting the opponents attack without breaking their momentum, and altering their line of movement in order to throw them.

Shime Waza

Strangulations and chokes when used correctly are a brutally effective way of eliminating a threat very quickly.* The word Shime or Jime is normally associated with these strangulations when in the context of martial arts, the word itself actually gives the idea of restriction, cut off, or closure, Shimekiri for example can refer to a deadline, also referred to as a cut off, or closing time. This makes perfect sense when we consider that Shime Waza work by cutting off the air or blood flow.

*It is important to only attempt these techniques when a qualified instructor, trained in resuscitation is present

What is interesting here, is that some joint locks may also be referred to as Shime, also bone or nerve attacks depending how they are performed may also be referred to as Shime. While I am mainly focusing on the strangulation or choking types here, I have included some of these other type of Shime in the examples.

With strangulation and choking the definitions are fairly simple. Where you are restricting the flow of blood through the neck to the brain, you are strangling your opponent. Where you are restricting the airflow through the throat to the lungs, you are choking them.

Strangles are performed by compressing the carotid arteries and/or the jugular veins, restricting the flow of blood to the brain and therefore starving it of oxygen. When performed correctly unconsciousness can occur within a matter of seconds, with death not far behind.

Chokes on the other hand are performed by compressing the larynx or trachea, preventing the lungs from being able to draw in air, preventing breathing and starving the blood of oxygen. As with strangulations, when chokes are performed correctly unconsciousness and death can occur very quickly, although they will generally take slightly longer to take effect.

Some Shime Waza may accomplish both of these things at the same time, strangling and choking an opponent.

In practice, Shime waza should only really be used when your opponent is anchored in some way, usually on the ground. While they are often practiced in a standing position, and the photos in this book are from a standing position for easy demonstration, if they were applied in this way in real life your opponent may be able to escape, they may be able to strike you, throw you, or even apply a Shime of their own. This is an important point to consider when practicing Shime Waza.

Generally these will be performed in one of three ways; by using your opponent's clothes to strangle or choke them, as a lever, or by applying a naked strangle or choke.

We will now look at some examples of these;

Using clothes to strangle / choke

In this example, Uke's collar is being pulled tightly against the side of the neck, compressing the carotid artery and jugular vein. At the same time, the crossed arms are pressing against the other side of Uke's neck, preventing them from being able to pull away from the choke.

Here the Shime is being applied in the same way with the collar being pulled against the side of the neck, but the grip is one handed. In the picture while the right hand is pulling the collar tight, the left arm is tucked under Uke's armpit restricting their movement while the hand is pressing against the back of the neck to prevent Uke from pulling away from the strangle.

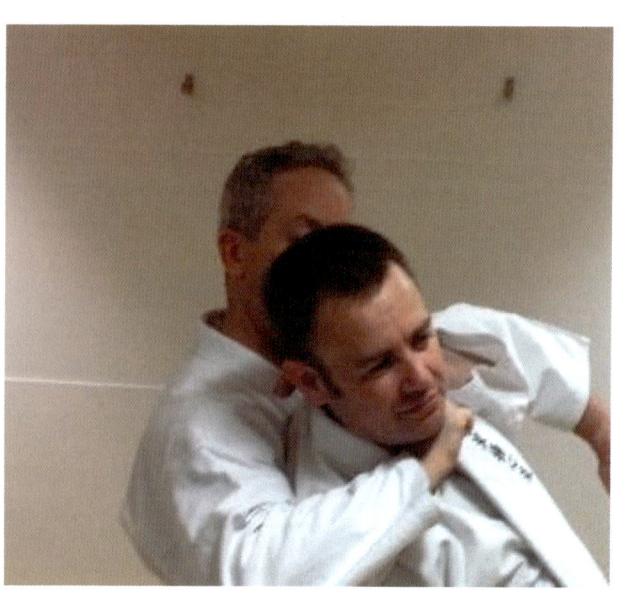

Using Clothes as a Lever

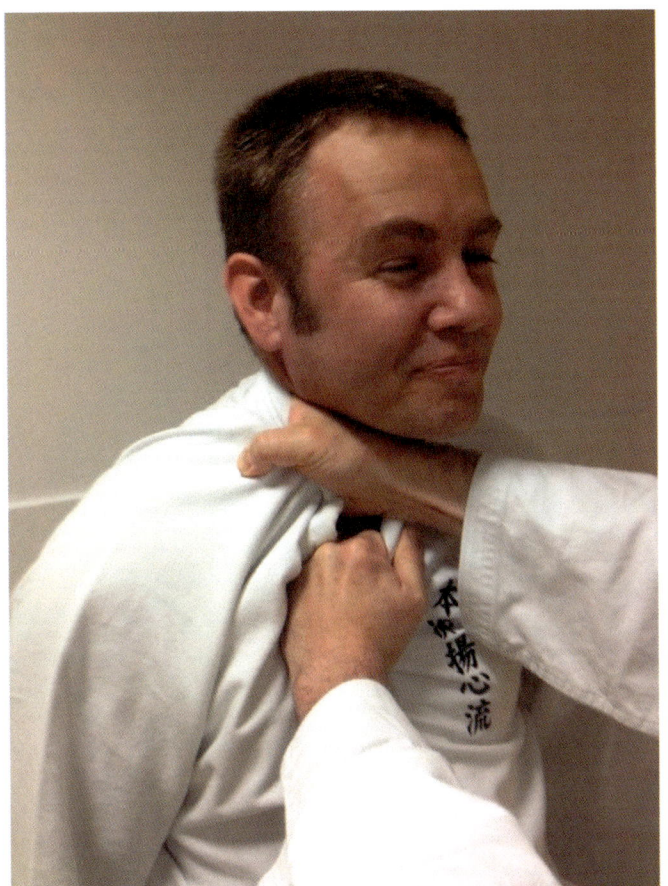

Here a Shime is being applied to the side of the neck to compress the carotid artery and jugular vein. Instead of using the collar to apply the strangle, the compression is created by pressing your knuckles into the side of the neck, using Uke's collar to anchor your hand in place. Your other hand pulls the other side of the collar tight in order to prevent Uke from pulling away from the Shime, as before.

Here the Shime is being applied in the same way as above, however instead of the knuckles pressing the neck to strangle, the bones of the wrist are used to press and crush the trachea.

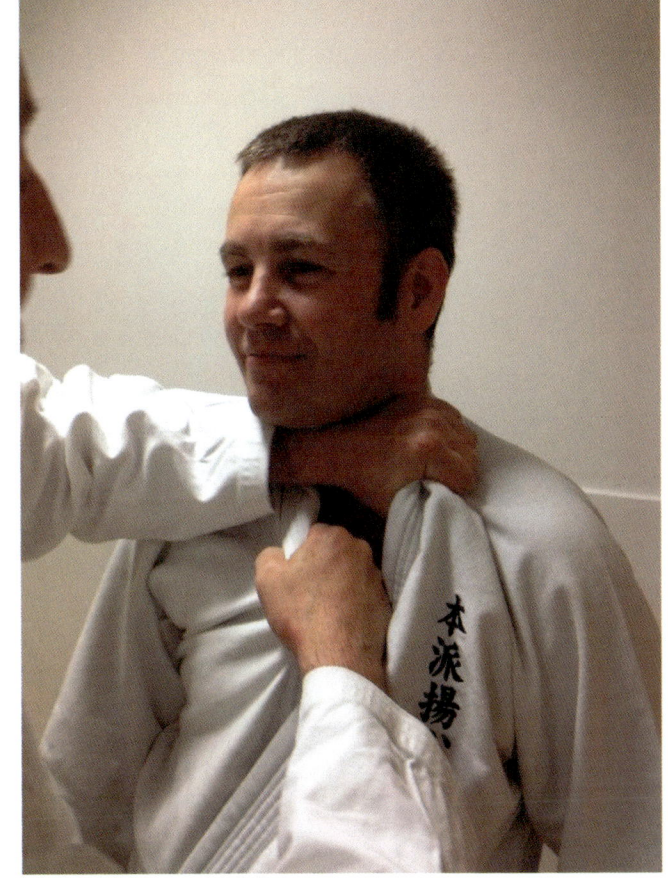

Naked Strangle / Choke

This type of Shime is referred to as Hadaka Jime (naked strangle/choke) as it can be applied without using Uke's clothing.

This can be applied as a strangle or choke purely dependent on the angle at which you apply the Shime.

The bones of the wrist are used to apply pressure, while the other hand provides additional compression, and the shoulder prevents Uke from pulling away, the head could also be used here to push Uke's head forward creating an even tighter strangle.

There are also alternative versions of this technique often seen in wrestling and grappling competitions. Clamping the hand applying the Shime into the inside of the opposite elbow, and placing that hand on the back of the head.

Closing

I hope you have enjoyed reading, and found some insight into this Martial Art which is so much a part of my life.

This has been fairly brief introduction into some of the main concepts that combine to make Jujutsu what it is.

If anyone would like to explore any of these concepts further, our doors are open to you.

Thank you

Guy

Glossary of Terms

Atemi	Striking
Bojutsu	Stick Method
Budo	Martial Way
Budoka	Person who follows the Martial Way
Bujutsu	Martial Method
Daisho	Pair of Swords as worn by Samurai
Dojo	Place for training
Fudoshin	Immovable Mind
Gaeshi	Change, Reverse
Gendai	Modern
Goshinjutsu	Self Defence Method
Gyaku	Twist, Reverse
Ha	Branch
Henka	Variation
Hyoho	Strategy
Iaido	Way of Drawing and Cutting
Irimi	Entering, Moving in
Jime (Shime)	Strangulation, Restriction
Judo	Way of Suppleness
Jujutsu	Supple Method
Kamae	Posture
Kanji	Japanese writing characters
Kata	Form
Keiko	Training
Kendo	Way of the Sword
Kenjutsu	Sword Method
Kobushi	Ancient Warrior
Kokusai	International
Koryu	Ancient Flow
Kote	Wrist
Kuzushi	Structure Break, Unbalance
Maai	Distance, Space Between
Mae	Front
Meiji	Period of Japanese History
Menkyo Kaiden	Certificate of Full Transmission
Metsuke	Piercing Eyes
Musha Shugyo	Pilgrimage of Training
Mushin	No Mind

Nagashi/Nagare	Flow
Nage	Throwing
Naginatajutsu	Halberd Method
Newaza	Ground Technique
Nihonto	Japanese Sword
Reiho	Bowing
Renmei	Federation
Ryu	Flow, School
Samurai	Japanese Warrior
Saya	Scabbard
Sensei	Teacher
Shime	Strangulation, Restriction
Soke	Head of Ryu, Inheritor
Taijutsu	Body Method
Te no Uchi	Hand Technique
Tori (Torime)	Person Performing Technique
Uke (Ukemi)	Person Receiving Technique
Ushiro	Behind
Waza	Technique
Yoshin	Spirit/Heart/Mind of the Willow
Zanshin	Remaining Mind

References

Hagakure, The Book of the Samurai – Yamamoto Tsunetomo (Translated by William Scott Wilson)

KJJR Jujutsu Vol. 1 – Tanemura Shoto

Asayama Ichiden Ryu Taijutsu – Iwaki Hideo (Translated by Masayo Jennings and Jason Jennings)

Go Rin no Sho, The Book of Five Rings – Miyamoto Musashi

Fundamental Kendo – All Japan Kendo Federation

Daito-Ryu Aikijujutsu, Hiden Mokuroku: Ikkajo – Kondo Katsuyuki

Secret Tactics, Lessons from the Great Masters of Martial Arts – Tabata Kazumi

Takagi-Ryu, Chugokui Mokuroku – Dr S Greenfield

Takagi Oriemon, Budo Hero of Shiroishi – Mamiya Hyoemon (Translated by Manaka Unsui)

Takagi Yoshin Ryu, Taijutsu no Kata – Carsten Kuhn

http://www.takenouchiryu.com/ - Takenouchi Ryu Official Website

http://motohayoshinryu.org – Motoha Yoshin Ryu Official Website

.

Printed in Great Britain
by Amazon